BRITISH RAIL SCRAPBOOK 1948

John Adams & Patrick Whitehouse

LONDON

IAN ALLAN LTD

A blue 'King', No 6016 *King Edward V* takes an up Wolverhampton-Birmingham-London (Paddington) express through the cuttings between Rowington and Hatton in September 1948. Colourviews Picture Library.

First published 1976

ISBN 0 7110 0693 8

Published by Ian Allan Ltd, Shepperton, Surrey, and printed in the United Kingdom by Ian Allan Printing Ltd.

THE RAILWAY ENTHUSIAST'S YEAR 1948

January 1, 1948 — funeral of GWR, LMS, LNER and SR, and birthday of the British Transport Commission as corporate overlord of the country's railways, public road transport, docks, canals and London Transport. Within the BTC the railways were now to be run by the Railway Executive, its first chairman the former Southern Railway General Manager, Sir Eustace Missenden (the job had been offered first to Sir James Milne of the Great Western, who declined it).

It choked some of the brotherhood. 'Even this book has turned Labour and talks of Southern Region and suchlike', one shocked Surrey subscriber remonstrated with the *Railway Magazine*. But railwaymen were basking in the millenium — or so they thought then, for by the year's end the NUR was complaining that 'centralised direction stultifies enterprise'. The first Sunday in January had been proclaimed Railway Sunday by the old Labour newspaper, the *Daily Herald*, and there was a move to enshrine it in the calendar for evermore. For months to come cartoonists and comedians were to play endless and ever more tedious variations on the theme of 'They're our railways now'.

How the new Executive would paint its trains was the major preoccupation of most enthusiasts. Pretty soon any depot with paint, brushes and an employee with signwriting pretensions was busy effacing evidence of previous ownership and slapping on 'British Railways' and E, M, S or W prefixes to rolling stock numbers, much as they pleased so far as style was concerned (some zealot at one stage ordered removal of pre-grouping nomenclature from locomotive building plates, but this lunacy was soon stopped). Then authority took a firmer grip and by the end of January we were offered samples of new official colour schemes.

On January 30 a parade at London's Kensington Olympia (or Addison Road, as it was still known then) presented four Stanier Class 5 4-6-0s in experimental shades: No 4762 in Southern malachite green; No 4763 in LNER green; No 4764 in GWR green; and No 5292 in the old LNWR lined black. Also on show was SR electric locomotive No CC2 in pale blue with silver lining. The *Railway Gazette* was pressing for a standardised Post Office red livery, but the Ex-

ecutive preferred more originality. By mid-February it made its provisional choice and on April 6 another review was staged, this time at Marylebone. By this time, too, the Executive had fixed its five-digit engine renumbering scheme, so some of the showpieces were carrying new smokebox numberplates. They comprised: Class A3 Pacific No 60091 *Captain Cuttle* in royal blue for major passenger engines; Class B17 4-6-0 No 61661 *Sheffield Wednesday* in light green, for other passenger engines; and Class 5 4-6-0 No 45292 in ex-LNWR lined black, intended for all other steam power.

All electric locomotives and multiple-units were to be malachite green, and locomotive-hauled non-corridor stock maroon, but the Executive was havering over a corridor stock style. It decided at first to give the country a choice of GW chocolate-and-cream and a bastardised LNWR coach livery which the *Times* scorned on sight as 'plum-and-spilt-milk', a disparagement that stuck throughout its brief life. At the end of May set trains in the new styles were put on nominated services in each Region and the public was urged to write its preferences to the Executive, but only a thousand or so bothered. (At the same time, incidentally, several East Coast train-sets were splashed with more fresh colours when the pre-war LNER streamliner sets, still in pre-1939 two-tone blue, were withdrawn from store and distributed for everyday use; even the cross-country York-Yarmouth and Manchester-Cleethorpes services got an articulated pair apiece).

Nationalisation had dawned on a period of considerable locomotive interest. The LMS was completing its last pair of Pacifics. Nos 6256 *Sir William A. Stanier FRS* and 6257 *City of Salford*, and simultaneously the country's first main-line diesel-electric, the 1,600hp No 10000. On January 14 and 15 the latter made its Midland line debut on dynamometer car trials with a 393ton train from St Pancras to Manchester and back on 'Jubilee' 4-6-0 timings, which it observed with ease; after a period for crew training, it began regular service on the 8.55 am Derby-St Pancras and 2.15pm back from February 23. The last new engine to emerge from Crewe under LMS ownership had been the first non-standard

Stanier Class 5, No 4767 with Stephenson valve gear; with 1948 came the first of the Caprotti valve gear 4-6-0s, No 4748. Meanwhile more of the orthodox Class 5 4-6-0s were coming off the production lines at both Crewe and Horwich. The last months of 1947 had revealed the three Ivatt light six-coupled designs, the Class 4 2-6-0 No 3000, Class 2 2-6-0 No 6400 and Class 2 2-6-2T No 1200; Horwich was to be busy proliferating the first during 1948, Crewe the other two. Derby's new steam construction was concentrated on Class 4 2-6-4Ts. On the rebuilding side, Crewe still had a few streamlined Pacifics to de-frock (only one streamliner, No 6243, was left by the year's end) and more 'Royal Scots' and 'Patriots' to convert with taper boilers.

On the LNER, No 525, Peppercorn's first Class A2 Pacific, named in his honour, had appeared late in 1947 and Doncaster was building more of the class as 1948 opened; the first Peppercorn A1 followed in August. Darlington works was engaged on Class L1 2-6-4Ts and the North British Loco Co was taking the B1 4-6-0 class past the century mark. Swindon entered 1948 completing a batch of Class 2251 0-6-0s in the 32XX series and 10 'Hall' 4-6-0s, then turned to 20 more 'Castle' 4-6-0s, Nos 7008-27, and more 0-6-0 pannier tanks. On the Southern, Brighton works was building more 'Battle of Britain' Pacifics, Eastleigh was tooling up for the final batch of 10 'Merchant Navy' Pacifics and the back-room boys were furtively hatching Bulleid's mysterious 'Leader'.

The pace of return to pre-1939 train service standards was dictated by coal scarcity as much as anything; the best grades were being appropriated for export and BR was left with the rubble. The shortage had persuaded the Government in late 1946 to order a massive coal/oil-burning conversion of 1,229 engines, ranging from 'West Country' Pacifics and 'King Arthur' 4-6-0s on the Southern to Garratts, ex-LNW 0-8-0s and Stanier 2-8-0s — in total, no fewer than 420 of the last two classes — on the London Midland. Money was ploughed into storage and fuelling plant, but meantime the balance of cost and availability was reversing in coal's favour; early in 1948 the scheme was called off after only 93 engines had been converted, but by then some £3 million had been wasted on it. Practically all the 93 were re-converted to coal burning before 1948 was out.

To conserve coal the Government had also enforced savage train service cuts in 1947. Almost all cross-country expresses had been axed as well as several into and out of London, startlingly headed by the 'Cornish Riviera Limited' in each direction. The Ministry of Transport warmed February 1948 a little by announcing that this year the only constraint on BR's summer service planning would be traction and rolling stock resources. And on February 16 normalcy seem-

ed another tiny stride closer with the restoration of the 'Royal Scot' title to the 10 o'clocks from Euston and Glasgow Central; it was the first LMS train name to be revived since the war.

Extinction of the steam-powered forerunner of today's diesel railcar was a feature of February's withdrawals from stock. Steam railcars had their first vogue at the start of the century, but in those days the power plant was small, conventional steam locomotives, sometimes articulated to a coach body, sometimes built into it; the GWR was particularly taken by the concept and built over 100. The railcar came back into fashion in the late 1920s, but this time most were powered by a high-speed geared engine taking steam from a high-pressure water-tube boiler. Sentinel and Clayton were the principal practitioners of this art and the LNER the major customer, with 90 railcars. Liveried green and white, they all bore racy stage-coach names (and each had the history of its forerunner displayed on a panel inside the saloon). Last to go was *Hope*, from Wetherby.

Some of the more significant classes to have their final survivors scrapped in February were the ex-North Eastern Class C6 4-4-2 (Nos 2933/7) and D17/2 4-4-0 Nos 2111/2, and — on the Western — the ex-Port Talbot Railway 0-8-2T (No 1358), an imposing quintet that once operated Duffryn Yard; three of them had been built by Sharp Stewart in 1901 and two in the USA in 1899. At the end of March the LMR condemned the last Glasgow & South Western engine in its stock, 0-6-2T No 16905. A unique modification completed in March was the equipment of SR 'Merchant Navy' Pacific No 21C5 *Canadian Pacific* with a mechanical stoker.

The first serious accident of the year hit the LMS just after midnight on April 17. At the approach to Winsford station, about 8 miles north of Crewe, the stationary 5.40 pm Glasgow-Euston, headed by 'Princess Royal' Pacific No 6207, was run into by 'Duchess' Pacific No 6251 on the following 6.25 pm Glasgow-Euston Postal. The 5.40's guard had got about ¼ mile to the rear of his train with a red lamp and laid detonators by the time the Postal came on the scene, so that No 6251's driver had pulled up to 45mph at the moment of collision. Fortunately, too, No 6207's driver had lifted his brakes, but even so the impact was fierce enough to destroy 16 lives in the last two coaches of the 5.40.

The press took off on characteristic flights of fancy when the 5.40 was found to have been stopped by a leave-going soldier pulling the communication cord because Winsford was his home town. The real culprit was the Winsford Station signalman; busy warming his evening meal, he thought the 5.40 must have passed him un-noticed, mis-reported it forward as 'out of section', then cleared the road for the Postal into the

Above: The last-but-one Stanier Pacific No 46256 *Sir William Stanier FRS* at Rugby in 1948, the year she was built.
Photo: J. M. Jarvis.

Below: The then new LMR diesel-electric locomotive No 10001 (twin to No 10000—this second engine was completed in mid-1948) on Bushey troughs with the down "Manxman".
Colourviews Picture Library.

back of it. Double track at this point, the main line was impassable for 20hr. Most expresses were diverted from Crewe via Chester (where reversal and engine change were necessary) to Halton Junction for Liverpool or Warrington for the north, but some took the more motive power-restrictive route via Manchester London Road Junction, the MSJA line, Ordsall Lane, Eccles Junction and Tyldesley to Wigan.

The LMR suffered another catastrophe on May 18 when 'Jubilee' 4-6-0s Nos 5605 and 5609, making 60-65mph on the 11.45am St Pancras-Bradford, hit a stretch of track distorted by hot sun near Wath Road Junction. The train engine toppled over, killing its driver, and the first few coaches were horribly jack-knifed down a 30ft embankment, fatally injuring seven passengers.

Since April 19 we had been absorbed by *the* locomotive event of the year — possibly of the decade: the Locomotive Exchanges. The trials continued until early September and many were the relatives untimely buried to get train-loggers time off for the unrepeatable opportunities to measure A4, 'Duchess', 'Merchant Navy' and 'King' against each other on the same routes and trains. A rebuilt 'Royal Scot' was pitched in amongst these Class 8 engines — but not a 'Castle', to the chagrin of Swindon's faithful. LNER devotees were just as incensed that no Class V2 2-6-2 — 'the engine that won the war' to many — had been excluded from the mixed-traffic contestants, which comprised a Bulleid 'West Country' Pacific, Stanier Class 5 4-6-0, Thompson Class B1 4-6-0 and Collett 'Hall' 4-6-0. For freight haulage, Western 28XX, LM 8F and ER Class O1 2-8-0s were set against the Riddles WD 2-8-0 and 2-10-0.

The 'King's' ventures abroad were restricted to the Kings Cross-Leeds test track, because of clearance problems; for similar reasons the WR 'Hall' could not operate in Scotland or on the Southern, nor the 28XX 2-8-0 on the LMR. The Southern Pacifics involved had to borrow LMR tenders for the trials, because their own had no water pick-up scoops. Conversely, because the Southern lacked track troughs and their normal tenders had comparatively limited water space, the LMR Pacific and 'Royal Scot' had to switch to eight-wheel WD 2-8-0 tenders with 1,000gal extra capacity for their Southern trips.

The express engines competed on the 10 am Euston-Carlisle and 12.55 pm back, the 1.10 pm Kings Cross-Leeds and 7.50 am back, the 1.30 pm Paddington-Plymouth and 8.30 am back, and the 10.50 am Waterloo-Exeter and 12.40 pm back. Test trains for the mixed traffic types were the 4 pm Perth-Inverness and 8.40 am back, the 10.15 am St Pancras-Manchester and 1.50 pm back, the 1.45 pm Bristol-Plymouth and 1.35 back, and the 10 am Marylebone-Manchester and 9.55 am back. The freight engines

were matched between Toton and Brent, London and Peterborough, London and South Wales and Bristol and Southampton.

It needed a book to describe and analyse the results fully: and the late Cecil J. Allen, dean of performance analysts, duly wrote it. That summer we had to be content with his first impressions. There was the 'unforgettable' experience of the 'Merchant Navy' *Belgian Marine* blasting up Shap with 530 tons and accelerating from 40 mph on the 1 in 125 to nearly 45mph on the 1 in 142, gaining 6½min on this stretch; the 'superb' exploits of the A4 *Seagull* on the WR, checked to 20mph at the foot of the 1 in 42 Hemerdon bank, but nevertheless lifting her 350ton train up the hill without a slip at a minimum of 18½mph, then accelerating the same load out of Taunton on almost level track to 75mph by Curry Rivell Junction; 'Royal Scot' *Queen's Westminster Rifleman's* 25½min time for the 27 unfriendly miles from Huntingdon to Hitchin with 545tons; and Stanier Pacific *City of Bradford's* charge of Dainton summit in 7½min from Newton Abbot. Most entertaining test of the whole series, unquestionably, was that of 'West Country' Pacific *Yeovil* on the Highland; the Bulleid engine romped so gaily up to 46mph on the 1 in 80 out of Blair Atholl that it winded its Caledonian 4-4-0 banker.

Overall, CJA handed his laurels to the Bulleid engines and the 'Royal Scot' for consistent merit. The 'King' had made its mark with the cleanest and smartest starts. The A4s had blotted their record three times with their besetting sin, overheated middle big-ends; worse still for the sensibilities of Gresley worshippers, the offender on two occasions was *Mallard,* which earlier in the year had been fitted with plaques recalling its record-breaking 126mph of July, 1938. The LMR Pacific nearly came to more serious grief for different reasons; on one trip its LM driver and the ER pilotman had a communication lapse approaching Peterborough, where the notorious curve was consequently taken at a speed that all but derailed the engine and wrought havoc in the train's kitchen car.

The summer timetables launched on May 31 restored non-stop Kings Cross-Edinburgh operation by the 'Flying Scotsman' and even the ladies' retiring room and cocktail lounge that were two hallmarks of the pre-war train; they were not the original pre-war vehicles, but adapted coaches in specially prepared, pressure-ventilated sets of the latest post-war Thompson stock, including a buffet as well as restaurant cars. Running time for the 392¼ miles was no less than 7hr 50min, representing a beggarly average of 50 mph. But even that was a whole hour faster than the 'Royal Scot's' Euston-Glasgow schedule.

It wasn't merely that engines and track were still

Above: With the pre-fix 'M' in front of her number, ex-LMS Class 3 No 741 is seen at Derby in January 1948.
Photo: J. M. Jarvis

Below: BR locomotive exchanges. Ex-Southern Railway Bulleid Pacific No 34006 *Bude* near Northwood on the Metropolitan & GC. Joint Line with a Manchester to Marylebone express on 1 June 1948.
Colourviews Picture Library.

dilapidated from war service, and that steaming could be wrecked by miserable coal. Operators were still hung over from the wartime laxity that excused ineptitude with a plea that vital freights had to go first — and anyway was your journey *really* necessary? The worst sinner was by common consent the LMR. During the Exchanges, for instance, Cecil J. Allen had slated LMR operators for money-wasting ruination of one test run by 'Merchant Navy' Pacific *Belgian Marine* because they stolidly left a sick Class 5 on a heavy RAF leave special labouring up the main line in front of the visitor all the way from Wigan to Leighton Buzzard, when at last they woke up and turned it on to the slow line. But by then the controllers had punished *Belgian Marine* with incessant signal checks totting up to 49 minutes' delay.

Sunday travel was especial purgatory, because of the frequent engineering possessions to catch up arrears of maintenance. The *Railway Gazette* quoted a typical summer Sunday run on the 10 am from Glasgow Central, which took over 11¼ hours to drag its weary passengers up to Euston. It had been heavily delayed by long stretches of single-line working round relaying north of Carlisle and north of Wigan, then had to divert from Stafford via Bushbury to Rugby because of more track work at Atherstone and trough renewal at Rugby. The same Pacific, No 46232 *Duchess of Montrose,* had been in charge throughout; unsurprisingly, it had been held for a further 18min re-coaling an empty tender at Rugby, as well as having had to stop for water at Wigan. One embittered monthly traveller on the 'Royal Scot', after 18 months without a punctual arrival and usually delays in excess of half-an-hour, suggested acidly that the LMR should publish only starting times with the qualification that 'by grace of God, the state of the track, the quality of the coal and the goodwill of all persons concerned, this train will reach its destination at least 12 hours after leaving.'

Two new named trains were added to the summer timetables. One was by titling a new 4.50 pm Marylebone-Bradford and the restored 10 am back the 'South Yorkshireman'. The other was the Southern's second post-war Pullman innovation, the summer-only 'Thanet Belle', between Victoria and Ramsgate; the previous summer had seen introduction of the Waterloo-Ilfracombe and Plymouth 'Devon Belle', tailed by a Pullman observation car, which was now back for its second summer season. On the East Coast route, the 'Queen of Scots' resumed its pre-war non-stop running between Kings Cross and Leeds — but on a lethargic 50.7mph average schedule half-an-hour slower than the pre-war 3hr 11min down and 3hr 10min up; in fact, the average journey time of all Kings Cross-Leeds expresses was no better than 4¼hr. Overall, the timetable still added up to little

more than three-fifths of the daily express train mileage run in the summer of 1935.

Back in 1948 closures and service withdrawals at each timetable change were usually modest and rated little attention in the railway press. Apart from a handful of stations, mainly on the LMR, the only significant changes announced for the end of May 1948 were withdrawal of the rump of the Liverpool Edge-Spellow service on the Alexandra Dock branch and of the solitary weekday train between Woodford & Hinton, on the ex-Great Central main line, and Byfield, on the former Stratford-on-Avon & Midland Junction line. This latter service was the lingering shadow of days when the 6.20 pm express from Marylebone used regularly to detach a slip-coach at Woodford for onward working to Stratford-on-Avon via the chord line to the SMJ at Woodford West Junction. At 93¼ miles this was the shortest rail route from London to Shakespeare's birthplace and for many years after 1902, when it launched its through service, the GCR exploited it to boast of the fastest time to Stratford. When it was finally withdrawn in February 1936 the through service from Marylebone still competed energetically in time with the GWR.

Two final points about the 1948 summer timetable books rate attention. Each Region contracted the size of its book drastically to a standard format based on the *Bradshaw* page size, with plain covers highlighting the new BR 'double-lozenge' totem in the new Regional colours — maroon for the LMR, dark blue for the ER, tangerine for the NER, light blue for the ScR, chocolate for the WR and malachite green for the SR.

And the price of the timetables? Three old pence a copy, or 1·25p in today's terms! As for rail fares in 1948, these are some third-class monthly return specimens: London-Birmingham £1·52½; London-Brighton 71p; London-Bristol £1·63; London-Edinburgh £5·37½; London-Leeds £2·52½; London-Nottingham £1·68; and London-Swansea £2·70.

In mid-April the Southern took in a couple of paying guests which made a mark on the Region's steam stud that lasted till its extinction. The newcomers were Class 4 2-6-4Ts Nos 42198/9, practically fresh from Derby works. No 42198 started off working the 10.54 am Waterloo-Basingstoke and 2.22 pm back in the last few days of April, then switched to Stewarts Lane for trials on South Eastern Section expresses between London termini and Tonbridge or Ashford. Eventually it joined its sister on the Oxted line, presaging the later adoption of the 2-6-4T as one of this route's staple types in its final years of steam working.

One of those self-generating enthusiast rumours was abroad that a Thompson L1 2-6-4T was to be tested on the Southern, but characteristically it was baseless. On their home ground the L1s were getting a mixed

Above: BR Locomotive exchanges. Ex-LNER A4
Pacific No 60034 *Lord Faringdon* on Bushey
troughs with the down "Royal Scot" on 17 May
1948.
Colourviews Picture Library.

Below: Ex-Southern Railway Bulleid Pacific
No 34004 *Yeovil* piloting the 5.5 pm Euston to
Crewe and points north en route for the locomotive
exchange trials in Scotland on 2 July 1948.
Colourviews Picture Library.

press. Darlington crews who ran them in ex-works damned them as ungainly and cruelly uncomfortable, but down south Neasden crews admired the way their small driving wheels scurried up the Chiltern Hills. The Stratford engines were making a good fist of the Southend fast trains, and in mid-May one was put on the Whit-Friday 3.44 pm Liverpool Street-Yarmouth restaurant car express; another had been spotted on the 8.24 am and 5.54 pm Liverpool Street-Cambridge expresses on May 13, in the latter case gasping a bit for water as the 5.54 was first stop out at Audley End, not Bishops Stortford.

New styles and liveries were not the only transformation of the railway scene compared with 1939. Another was the knots — crowds even — of youngsters accumulating on main-line stations and at vantage trackside points. Before the war the railways had published little on their locomotives beyond lists of names and basic dimensional data; the only way to try and work out a full class list was by personal observation. Towards the end of the war the enterprising Ian Allan sensed the huge latent interest and produced his first locomotive ABCs, listing by number and class every engine in service. The response was immediate and overwhelming — at the peak of post-war steam interest, in fact, an aggregate of close on half-a-million *ABCs* in their six-monthly and various Regional editions were sold annually. 'Locospotting' became common parlance as well as a widespread hobby.

Some pre-war enthusiasts reacted rather like MCC members confronted by a pop festival on the Lords turf. By and large, locospotters of the late 1940s behaved angelically compared with the vandals of the 1970s — and would stand up well against some of the reckless trespassers one has seen on latter-day steam outings. However, at busy junctions their lemming-like rushes down the platform on the scent of a 'cop' could be at best a nuisance and at worst a hazard to both railwaymen and public. Notorious for this was Tamworth, with its continuous double feature of West Coast main line below and Derby-Birmingham-Bristol main line above; at peak traffic periods the station drew crowds that frequently made the stairs between the upper and lower level stations like the exits from a Manchester United Cuptie. Towards the end of May the LMR decided it had had enough, and Tamworth became the first station to be barred to locospotters.

One of the more romantic pre-grouping locomotive classes vanished in May and June with condemnation of the last two ex-LNWR 'George the Fifth' 4-4-0s, Nos 25350 and 25373 *Ptarmigan;* however, representatives of three other LNWR express passenger types were still alive — the last 'Claughton' 4-6-0, No 6004 (at Liverpool's Edge Hill shed), the last 'Precursor' 4-4-0 No 25297 *Sirocco* and three 'Prince of Wales'

4-6-0s, Nos 25648 *Queen of the Belgians*, 25673 *Lusitania* and 25752. At the same time the LMR began putting the torch to another celebrated pre-1923 class with the first withdrawals of Midland compound 4-4-0s, Nos 1002/29.

The Western Region still had over 30 active 'Bulldog' 4-4-0s. A number of them were at Newton Abbot, principally for employment as pilots over the South Devon banks and in Cornwall (in July No 3363 got as far east as Savernake piloting a 'Castle' on a Plymouth-Paddington express), but the summer service rostered one to wear express passenger headlamps regularly on its own once again. It was booked to work a Kingswear portion through to Exeter for association there with a Penzance portion to form the 3.30 pm express to Paddington. At the same time a shadow was cast over the 'Bulldogs'' future with the first posting of 'Manor' 4-6-0s to Newton Abbot and Laira sheds.

Midsummer brought fresh signs that Derby's latest mixed traffic designs would be standardised on more Regions than the LMR. On the Southern it was reported that Eastleigh works would drop a plan for 20 more Bulleid Class Q1 0-6-0s and build LM 2-6-4Ts instead. On the Eastern, Colwick received one each of the Ivatt Class 2 and 4 2-6-0s for ex-LNER line duties in the East Midlands; other examples of each class went to Stratford, on the GE line, for trials (which had no regular service outcome); and a Class 4 2-6-0 made its debut on a Kings Cross-Peterborough express freight in mid-July. In the North-East, two more Ivatt Class 2 2-6-0s arrived at Darlington to shake the grip of the ex-North Eastern Class J21 0-6-0s on the steeply graded Darlington-Kirkby Stephen-Penrith line.

We had an unpleasant reminder of the railways' still sadly run-down state on the early morning of July 17, when Class A2/1 Pacific No 60508 *Duke of Rothesay* emerged from New Southgate tunnel and, at the first piece of pointwork, strewed itself and the first coach of the 7.50 pm Edinburgh-Kings Cross all over the track; the fireman was killed, but happily no passengers. The cause of the accident was derailment of the Pacific's trailing bogie on a maladjusted rail joint within the tunnel. A contributory factor may have been speed between 65 and 70mph, whereas — we were grimly reminded at the official inquiry — the state of the track and shortage of permanent way staff still imposed a speed limit of 60mph all the way in from Hatfield to Kings Cross.

The ranks of what was to many minds Britain's most elegant express passenger locomotive line, the Atlantics, were shrinking. Most numerous were the Robinson survivors of the Great Central, eking out their last days in Lincolnshire; the Ivatt engines of the Great Northern were down to 10 and the ex-North

Above: The last two LNWR 'George the Fifth' class were withdrawn in 1948, Nos 25350 (formerly *India*) and 25373 *Ptarmigan;* the latter is seen here in Crewe works for her last repair on 31 May 1947. Photo: H. C. Casserley.

Below: With a cast-iron smokebox numberplate but the word "Southern" on her tender, ex LBSCR H2 class 4-4-2 No 32424 *Beachy Head* takes the through train from Brighton to Bournemouth past Millbrook, Southampton in July 1948. Photo: P. M. Alexander.

Eastern Atlantics to two C7s, both of which were to disappear by the year's end. Over on the Southern, though, the Brighton Atlantics had lost only two of their number, Class H1 Nos 2040/1 withdrawn in 1944 (but No 2040 was not cut up until early 1948). The H2s were revelling in an Indian summer. Decked out in post-war coats of malachite green, they were first choice engines for the Victoria-Newhaven boat trains and, as R. C. Riley has written in a survey of the class, 'in the skilful hands of Newhaven men who really knew how to handle them their performance was of a very high standard.' It needed to be, for these trains were generally grossing over 400 tons, swollen by Britons with new-found holiday cash and a cheap Newhaven-Dieppe fare to entice them across the Channel. The cramped shed layout at Newhaven dictated the size of engine usable on the boat trains and the only practical alternative to the 4-4-2s was the later and more potent 'Schools' 4-4-0; but when a pair of the latter were sent to Newhaven toward the end of 1948 the Atlantics still clung to a good deal of the work and never fully yielded the pass until the new SR electric locomotives were brought in the following May.

Only one Brighton Atlantic was forlornly in the doldrums, H1 No 2039 *Hartland Point*. In July, 1947 it had had its front end mutilated with a chain-driven sleeve-valve arrangement, outside steampipes and crude, rimless chimney as a guinea-pig for the almost science-fictional 'Leader' engines Bulleid was fashioning at Brighton works. No 2039 spent 1948 intermittently trundling out of Brighton works on short-range test trips and back in again for repairs or adjustments. Not one passenger or pound of freight did it haul all year.

In the second week of August torrential rainstorms lashed the North-East Coast and washed away seven bridges on the Berwick-Edinburgh main line. The day it happened, August 12, the down 'Flying Scotsman' was diverted from Newcastle with the aim of getting it to Edinburgh via the Waverley Route, but the unlucky train found that route cut by the time it got to Hawick. It was reversed to Carlisle to try the West Coast main line and eventually, after a shuffle and reversal through Dalry Road and Haymarket West, limped into Edinburgh Waverley at the ungodly hour of 3.51 am, 10 hours late.

For the next few days the 'Scotsman' made the exhausting detour via Carstairs and Carlisle both ways. Then the operators cut out the East Coast Route north of Shaftholme Junction and ran the express to and from Carlisle via Knottingley, Leeds and Ais Gill; the A4 ran through to Leeds and beyond the train had such unlikely power, captured in one historic photo, as ex-Midland 4-4-0 No 40459 and Class 5 4-6-0 No 45223. By August 17 sufficient flood damage had

been made good to allow resumption of non-stop running — not via the direct main line, but from Edinburgh south through Galashiels to St Boswells, then eastwards down the Tweed Valley through Kelso to rejoin the usual path at Tweedmouth. The 'Scotsman' could now be returned to within 90min of its normal 7hr 50min timing; when a special emergency timetable was adopted on September 6, the difference was reduced to an even hour.

The train was not strictly non-stop as the schedule provided for a pause at Galashiels to take water and, if necessary, a pilot before assaulting the fierce 7½-mile climb at 1 in 70 to Falahill summit, 900ft up between the Moorfoot and Lammermuir Hills. Nevertheless one redoubtable Haymarket driver, Jimmy Swan, spurned the Galashiels stop and made a truly non-stop run in each direction more than once, establishing a new British record. The normal East Coast Route was reopened to freight on October 25 and to all traffic on November 1.

The summer also had a narrow-gauge casualty. Erosion of its track-bed had hammered the last nails into the coffin of the 2ft 3in-gauge Corris Railway, opened in 1859 to move slate down to the River Dovey and taken over by the GWR in 1930. The GWR had promptly axed its passenger service but continued goods traffic until August 20, 1948.

More cross-country trains were restored to the winter timetables, including the Brighton/Margate-Birkenhead, Bournemouth-Birkenhead and Liverpool-Harwich, and a regular interval service was put on between Glasgow Queen Street and Edinburgh Waverley. Two more new named trains were inaugurated, the Liverpool Street-Norwich 'Norfolkman' and the Kings Cross-Newcastle 'Tees-Tyne Pullman', complete with a Pullman refurbished as 'The Hadrian Bar', and running roughly in the path of the pre-war 'Silver Jubilee' streamliner. But the Pullman's Kings Cross-Newcastle schedule was a sluggish 5hr 20min with a Darlington stop, despite a formation of only eight cars. In fact, the timetables were still without a single mile-a-minute schedule. The best on offer were six 58.8mph bookings between Darlington and York, 57.4mph by the southbound 'West Coast Postal' between Forfar and Perth, 57.3mph by the 8.10 am Windermere-Manchester from Oxenholme to Lancaster, and 56.7mph by the 'South Yorksireman' — with a B1 4-6-0! — between Aylesbury and Leicester. Only on stretches of the Western was the permitted maximum speed as high as 85mph.

Still 5000 coaches short compared with 1939, BR could only offer about 83 per cent of the pre-war daily mileage in its winter service. But already road competition was biting hard, the railways were losing traffic and failure to meet the year's £28m interest charges was forecast. The *Economist* was more prescient than

Gresley A4 Pacific No 60028 *Walter K Whigham* in experimental blue livery at Grantham in June 1948.
Photo: J. M. Jarvis.

13

Above: Ex GWR Dean Goods No 2543 on a Mid-Wales local train in summer 1948.
Photo: P. M. Alexander.

the railway press; the situation was 'of profound importance for the future of the British economy', it warned, in contrast to the *Railway Gazette's* bland 'Would even a £28m loss on the railways be such a serious matter in the first year of nationalisation?'

The second of the pioneer LMR 1600hp diesel-electric twins, No 10001, had been completed in mid-year and on October 5 the pair began multiple-unit working on Euston-Glasgow expresses. Another important event, on October 19, was the formal opening of the Rugby stationary testing plant by the Minister of Transport, Mr Alfred Barnes. In honour of the man who campaigned most forcefully for this national facility, the engine displayed to the guests on the rollers was Class A4 No 60007 *Sir Nigel Gresley*.

The LMR gladdened the older generation with an announcement that it was going to revive old LNWR names for eight rebuilt 'Patriot' 4-6-0s, starting with No 45545 *Planet*. Sadly, this was the only name applied and the others — *Vulcan, Goliath, Courier, Velocipede, Champion, Dragon* and *Harlequin* — were never cast.

Another far-famed pre-war service to be revived, on December 6, was the Cambridge 'Beer Trains' — the light buffet car expresses between Cambridge and Kings Cross on which the Ivatt Atlantics had been able in the late 1930s to re-live a little of their pre-Pacific past. But the 1948 end-to-end times were 82-92min, instead of the 1939 72-75min, and the power now B1 or B17 4-6-0s. Talking of the B17s, the two allocated to the pre-war 'East Anglian', Nos 61659/70, were still streamlined in 1948 and the first of these two, re-allocated to Cambridge, had made its debut in Kings Cross on October 11. Ex-GE Class D16 4-4-0s still appeared in Kings Cross from time to time on the Cambridge trains.

The breaking down of pre-1948 boundaries was patent in Birmingham from November 1 with the daily arrival of a Class B1 4-6-0 at New Street — the first through working of an ex-LNER engine to this station. It arose from extension of the Birmingham-Lincoln daily service to and from Grimsby and Cleethorpes.

Among the more interesting locomotive classes to be extinguished in the second half of the year were the country's last 0-4-2 tender engines, Nos 627/9 of the Southern's Class A12; as already foreshadowed, the last North Eastern Atlantic, C7 No 2970; the last of the 10 little Great Eastern 45¾ton branch-line Class F7 2-4-2Ts, nicknamed the 'Crystal Palace' class because of the massive side-window cabs that dwarfed their tiny boilers, and of which the survivors had ended their careers on the Great North of Scotland; the ex-Caledonian 'Dunalastair' IV' 4-4-0; the two Metropolitan Railway named 0-6-4Ts, which became LNER Class M2; the last ex-LNWR steam rail motor, which had finished up on the Beatock-Moffat branch; and the original Gresley Pacific with the final conversion of Nos 60068 *Sir Visto* from Class A10 to Class A3.

The year ended with a Railway Executive announcement that it had settled its new rolling stock liveries. The principal express passenger classes were to retain blue livery, but of a lighter shade than the experimental choice, and with black and white lining instead of the initial yellow. Instead of the light green tried at first, dark Brunswick Green with black and orange lining would be applied to other express passenger and leading mixed traffic types. For the rest the livery would be black, with red, cream and grey lining. The locomotives were also acquiring a new embellishment on tender or tank sides — the lion and wheel emblem of BR, already dubbed the 'ferret and dartboard' by many of us. Both experimental main-line coach liveries were rejected — to the disgust of many in the case of chocolate and cream — and carmine and cream selected.

Ex-LMS 'Patriot' No 45531 *Sir Frederick Harrison* rebuilt with taper boiler, new cylinders and double chimney seen at Derby in May 1948, resplendent in experimental LNER green livery.

Photo: J. M. Jarvis.

15

Above: A class which became extinct in 1948 was the Metropolitan 0-6-4T. This picture of old No 97 *Brill* was taken in May 1937 at Aylesbury.
Photo: John Adams

Below: Eleventh-hour test: British Railways Locomotive Testing Station at Rugby was officially opened by the then Minister of Transport Rt. Hon. Alfred Barnes, PC, MP on 19 October 1948. Originally planned as an LMS/LNER joint venture this plant had a short life but its shell still stands adjacent to the long and now lifeless GC bridge crossing the LNW tracks south of Rugby station. The locomotive on "test" on the Opening Day was A4 No 60007 *Sir Nigel Gresley*.
Photo: British Railways.

Above: An oddity taken over by the Railway Executive was the East Kent Railway — a Colonel Stephens enterprise. Here is an ex SE&CR Wainwright C class 0-6-0 (late EKR) standing at Shepherdswell sporting her new cast smokebox numberplate as BR No 31065.
Photo: P. J. Lynch.

Overleaf: Ex-LNER A4 Pacific No 60007 *Sir Nigel Gresley* outside the Rugby Locomotive Testing Station the day before the official opening.
Photo: J. M. Jarvis.

Above: This Birmingham Division local train of the GWR seen on Rowington water troughs near Lapworth, was to remain almost unchanged for another eight years until the coming of the dmus. Under the new numbering scheme ex-Great Western engines retained their brass and cast-iron side number plates, but exchanged a painted buffer beam number for a cast-iron smokebox one. Colourviews Picture Library.

Below: LNER 'Football' ('Sandringham' class) 4-6-0 *Sheffield Wednesday* as Railway Executive/British Railways No 61661 in experimental light green livery at Liverpool Street station in January 1948.
Photo: British Railways.

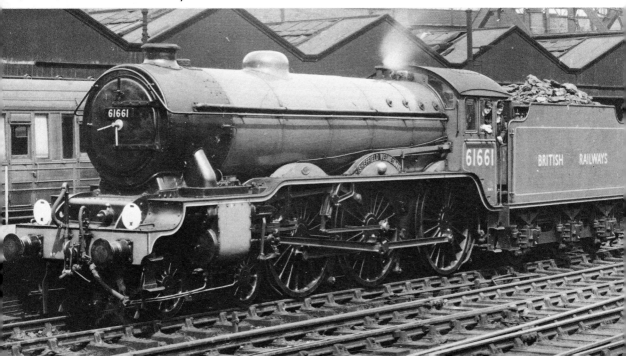

Fowler 2-6-2T No 40040 emerged from Derby Works in 1948 complete with push-and-pull gear, condensing apparatus for working over London's Underground system and a cast-iron smokebox plate carrying the 40000 prefix denoting its new Region under nationalisation. This was in January when no one really knew how the legend of the Executive was to be proclaimed and the lesser evil was to keep the old LMS initials.
Photo: J. M. Jarvis

G.W.R. Castle 4-6-0 No 7010 *Avondale Castle,* one of the post-war Hawksworth batch, in 1948. This loco was the first 'Castle' to be painted in Railway Executive apple green, lined red, cream and grey. The engine was later (12 June 1956) repainted in GWR-style livery except for boiler bands, Belpaire firebox, cab panel and smokebox number.
Photo: G. Wheeler.

The new nationalised railway was very quick to mark its own property and each new Region equally keen to do the same. Prior to the new numbering system becoming official some engines carried the Regional prefix on their cabsides or bufferbeams. This Stanier 'Black Five' was outshopped new from Crewe complete with cast smokebox plate M 4750. The photograph was taken at New Street Station, Birmingham on 25 March 1948.
Photo: C. F. H. Oldham.

Above: The livery chosen for third-rank passenger and mixed traffic engines was similar to that of the LNWR. Just as, in 1923, the "George the Fifths" looked out of place in Midland red, this livery scarcely suited Midland-designed black compounds.
R. G. Jarvis

Below: Before long the words British Railways on locomotive tenders and tank sides gave way to the first "emblem" of a lion across a wheel. Here is re-boilered 'Royal Scot' as BR No 46118 *Royal Welch Fusileer,* newly painted at Crewe.
Photo: Colourviews Picture Library.

Western in the Birmingham Division (1) Standard GWR 2-6-2T No 5161 leaves Knowle & Dorridge station on the up main line with a Snow Hill to Leamington local on 27 March 1948. The engine is still in full GWR livery.
Photo: C. F. H. Oldham.

Above: Western in the Birmingham Division (2) New Hawksworth modified Hall No 6986 *Rydal Hall* with a Leamington suburban train at Bentley Heath crossing on 29 March 1948. Note the early period Birmingham Division local set of four coaches with snap-down handles — you had to lean out of the window to close the door. Note the wording 'British Railways' on the tender in full GWR-type lettering. Photo: C. F. H. Oldham.

Above right: Western in the Birmingham Division (3) 'County' class 4-6-0 No 1024 *County of Pembroke* approaching Bentley Heath crossing with a down fast on 25 March 1948. The engine is in full GWR livery as are the coaches — note coat of arms on tender and coach panels. Photo: C. F. H. Oldham.

Right: Western in the Birmingham Division (4) Standard GWR 2-6-2T No 5187 at Birmingham Snow Hill on 23 April 1948. Note the absence of cast-iron numberplate numbers on bufferbeam in accordance with GWR practice and tank side lettering 'British Railways' in standard GWR-type lettering. Photo: C. F. H. Oldham.

No. S2330 *Cudworth* of Southern Class N15X, which were built in 1914 for the LB&SCR to the designs of L. B. Billinton as Class L 4–6–4Ts.
Colourviews Picture Library

Like the Compounds, the ex-Midland Railway Class 2 4–4–0s never really looked right in pseudo-LNWR livery. No 40383 has just been outshopped from Derby Works in June 1948.

Photo: R. G. Jarvis.

Dean Goods 0-6-0 No 2323 at Portmadoc station on 24 September 1948. The engine is in full GWR livery with the lettering MCH on the framing adjacent to the buffer beam denoting its home shed, Machynlleth.
Photo: C. F. H. Oldham.

Below: GWR-built post-war 'Castle' class 4-6-0 No 7006 *Lydford Castle* with a Birmingham to Worcester local leaving Stratford-upon-Avon for Honeybourne on 2 October 1948. The engine is in what became semi-standard livery for the period, viz GWR but with the words British Railways on the tender.
Photo: C. F. H. Oldham.

Above: In the early days of her life Stanier 5MT No M 4748, the first of five engines with Caprotti valve gear and Timken roller bearings, seen at Derby in March 1948.
Photo: J. M. Jarvis.

Below: The same engine at Willesden on 4 March 1953.
Photo: A. T. H. Tayler.

Above: BR locomotive exchanges. Ex-LNER A4 Pacific No 60034 *Lord Faringdon* on Bushey troughs with the down 'Royal Scot' on 27 May 1948.
Colourviews Picture Library.

Below: BR Locomotive exchanges. Western Region No 6990 *Witherslack Hall,* still carrying the letters GW oh her tender, on the Metropolitan & GC Joint Line near Northwood with the 8.25 am from Manchester on 23 June 1948.
Colourviews Picture Library.

Above: BR locomotive exchanges. Ex-Southern Railway Bulleid Pacific No 34006 *Bude* near Rickmansworth with a Manchester to Marylebone express on 3 June 1948.
Colourviews Picture Library.

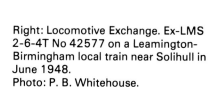

Right: Locomotive Exchange. Ex-LMS 2-6-4T No 42577 on a Leamington-Birmingham local train near Solihull in June 1948.
Photo: P. B. Whitehouse.

Right: Locomotive exchange 1948 (Perth-Inverness). At Perth on 15 July 1948, SR 'West Country' Pacific No 34004 *Yeovil* is waiting to leave with the 4 pm express to Inverness. A ''Caley'' 4-4-0 can be seen behind the SR Pacific. First vehicle of the train is the LNER dynamometer car.
Photo: Ian Allan Library.

Above: The first 'Castle' to be constructed under nationalisation No 7008 *Swansea Castle,* with a Birkenhead to Bournemouth express near Solihull.
Photo: C. F. H. Oldham.

Below: British Railways in South Devon — GWR 'Grange' class 4-6-0 No 6822 *Manton Grange* at Exeter St Davids with a local train for Torbay on 22 June 1948.
Photo: C. F. H. Oldham.

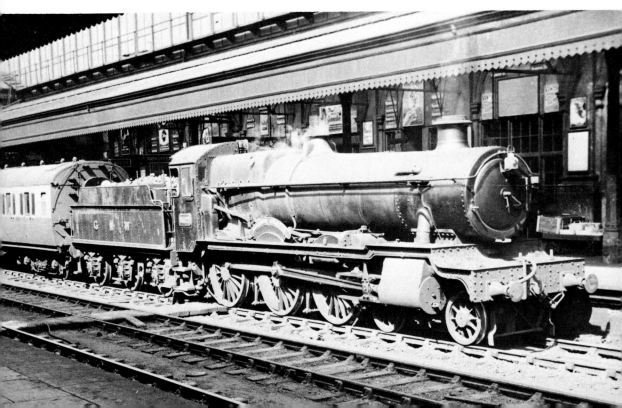

Above: Ex-Midland Railway Class 2 4-4-0 No 437, with disfiguring Stanier chimney, takes an up local over the main line.
Photo: P. M. Alexander.

Below: Still bearing Bulleid's numbering, 21C153 'Battle of Britain' class light Pacific *Sir Keith Park* heads a semi-fast.
Photo: P. M. Alexander

Britain's last 0-4-2 tender locomotives were Class A12 and these became extinct during 1948. Here is one of the last survivors, No 643, at Guildford in 1947.
Photo: P. M. Alexander.

Right: No 7013 *Bristol Castle* with Hawksworth straight-sided tender on Campden bank near Mickleton. Later, in 1952 this engine exchanged names and number plates with old No 4083 *Windsor Castle* for use on King George V's funeral train, the latter being in Swindon Works at the time.
Photo: C. F. H. Oldham.

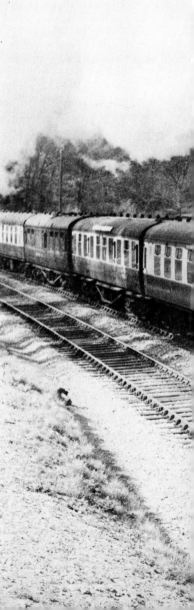

Below: Ex-GER 2-4-2T of 1909 as LNER Class F7 No 8304. These engines were Great Eastern class Y65 introduced by Holden in 1909. The class became extinct in 1948.
Photo: Colourviews Picture Library.

1948 saw the withdrawal of the first two Midland Compound 4-4-0s, Nos 1002/29. The former is shown here at the head of a Leeds to Morecambe express near Bell Busk.
Photo: Eric Treacy.

Above: At the end of its period of Southern Railway ownership the Isle of Wight system still ran the odd ex-LB & SCR 'Terrier' 0-6-0 tank. Here is No 13 *Carisbrooke* in lined SR livery. Seen at Newport in May 1936.
Photo: John Adams.

Below: Another "Terrier" still extant was K&ESR No 3 *Bodiam.* Taken into the Southern Region network this old Colonel Stephens line survived in part to become a preserved railway based on Tenterden. Here is No 3 freshly painted outside its shed at Rolvenden in May 1935.
Photo: John Adams.

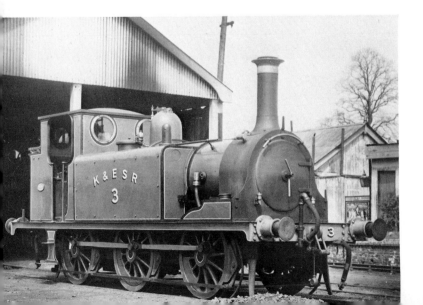

Right: The old Corris Railway was closed by the Western Region on 20 August 1948. Its two locomotives Nos 3 and 4 are awaiting disposal in the Corris station yard at Machynlleth. (They were finally purchased by the Talyllyn Railway Preservation Society). Photo: P. M. Alexander.

Below: One of the oddments to enter the books of the new Railway Executive was the one-time Cambrian, later Great Western 2ft 6in-gauge line from Welshpool to Llanfair Caereinion in Montgomeryshire. The locomotive stock consisted of two 0-6-0 tanks, Nos 822 *The Earl* and 823 *Countess*. The latter is seen here with the daily freight crossing Raven Square in November 1948. Photo: P. B. Whitehouse.

Top left: Northallerton, 19 May 1948. Class D20 4-4-0 No 2391 (Ex NER R class) is using the triangle to turn round after bringing in a train from Hartlepool.
Photo: P. M. Alexander.

Upper right: Ex-NBR D30 'Scott' class 4-4-0 No 2436 *Lord Glenvarloch* still in LNER livery on a Thornton Junction to Perth train at Perth in July 1948.
Photo: P. M. Alexander.

Left: In LNER livery, ex-NER D20 class 4-4-0 No 2395 leaves York with the 4.31 pm to Harrogate train on 21 May 1948.
Photo: P. M. Alexander.

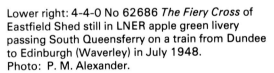

Lower right: 4-4-0 No 62686 *The Fiery Cross* of Eastfield Shed still in LNER apple green livery passing South Queensferry on a train from Dundee to Edinburgh (Waverley) in July 1948.
Photo: P. M. Alexander.

Lower left: An LNER 'Hunt' class 4-4-0 in full BR livery as No 62727 *The Quorn* on Crimple Viaduct near Harrogate on 21 May 1948.
Photo: P. M. Alexander.

Several of the ex-North London Railway 0-6-0 side tanks passed into the hands of British Railways — mostly based on the Cromford & High Peak system in Derbyshire. Such was LMS No 27509 seen here at Derby works and later to be re-numbered 58851.
Photo: J. M. Jarvis.

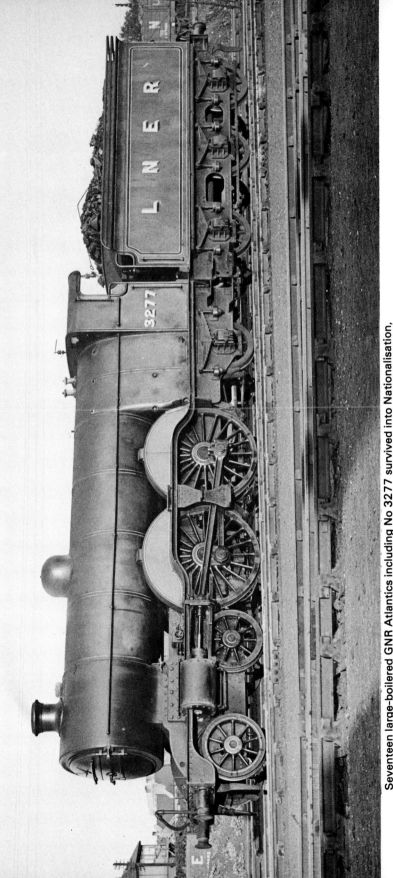

Seventeen large-boilered GNR Atlantics including No 3277 survived into Nationalisation, but only just — the last survivor went in 1950. No 251 is preserved in York Railway Museum.

Photo: John Adams.

Upper left: Ex LBSCR H2 class 4-4-2 with SR number 2423 *The Needles* on the 5.40 pm London Bridge-Brighton via Oxted, passing New Cross Gate on 1 July 1948.
Photo: P. M. Alexander.

Lower left: Experimental sleeve valves and gear of ex-LB&SCR 4-4-2 No 2039 *Hartland Point*. The motion of the valve was reciprocating and partly rotary (through about 30°). It was driven through rocking shafts from the inside motion of the engine. The cylinder diameter was reduced considerably to accommodate the valves.
Photo. P. Ransome-Wallis.

Below: Ex-Great Central Railway 4-4-2 No 6088 on a parcels train in 1933. This was one of the few remaining engines of the class to pass into BR ownership in 1948. Renumbered under the post war LNER scheme, she became No 2912 and 62912 successively.
Colourviews Picture Library.

Above: Ex-LSWR T9 class 4-4-0 No 713 (oil burning) with a train near Fareham on 25 September 1948.
Photo: P. M. Alexander.

Below: Bulleid light Pacific No 34036 (allotted the name *Westward Ho!*) converted for oil burning, near Fareham with the 8.10 am Bristol (Temple Meads) to Portsmouth on 25 September 1948.
Photo: P. M. Alexander.

Above: G.W.R. No 7003 *Elmley Castle* near Brinkworth, Wiltshire on the down "Pembroke Coast Express", introduced during the summer of 1948.
Photo: P. M. Alexander.

Below: Bulleid light Pacific No 21C152 *Lord Dowding,* still carrying her peculiar Southern number, heads the 12.50 pm Waterloo to the West through Weybridge on 20 September 1948.
Photo: P. M. Alexander.

Above: An as yet un-named Bulleid Pacific with Southern number 21C162 and old-type cab on the down "Thanet Belle" near Herne Bay.
Photo: P. Ransome-Wallis.

Below: A Horwich-designed "Crab" 2-6-0 No 42846, but with LMS still on her tender, climbs the Lickey Incline in May 1948.
Photo: P. B. Whitehouse.

Ex-LMS Beyer Garratt, No 47986 passing Barrow-on-Soar on a down freight to Toton Sidings during June 1948.
Photo: P. M. Alexander.

Upper left: Ex-LNER Class O2 2-8-0 No 3931 passing Lincoln Loco Depot on an up goods on 18 April 1948 with her old number but with British Railways on her tender.
Photo: P. M. Alexander.

Above: Ex-LSWR K10 class 4-4-0 as SR No 141 on the 6.42 am freight from Guildford to Godalming at Shalford Junction on 31 August 1948.
Photo: P. M. Alexander.

Lower left: Ex-LNER Class O2 2-8-0 No 63971 passing Lincoln Loco Depot on an up goods on the same date re-numbered and with British Railways on her tender.
Photo: P. M. Alexander.

Right: WD No 79309. Unlettered with regard to ownership and with an undecipherable number, an 'Austerity' 2-8-0 built for the Government during the war trundles a freight between Widney Manor and Knowle & Dorridge on 24 April 1948.
Photo: C. F. H. Oldham.

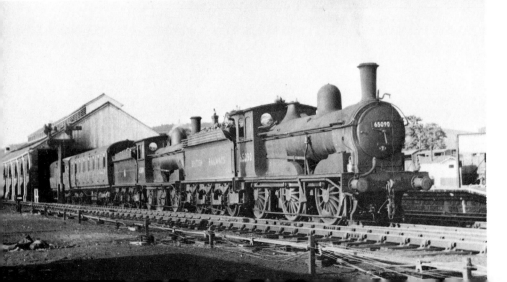

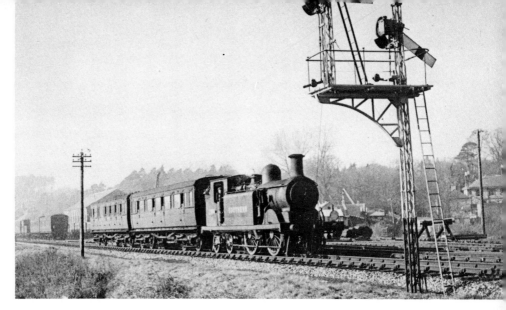

Upper left: Coalport station on the old LNWR branch from Wellington. An 18in goods ('Cauliflower') 0-6-0 prepares to depart with the afternoon train in June 1948.
Photo: P. B. Whitehouse.

Middle left: Aylesbury (LNW) branch train nearing Cheddington behind 'Coal Tank' No 58926 in November 1948.
Photo: P. B. Whitehouse.

Lower left: The ex-North Eastern Railway's J21 class 0-6-0s were the mainstay of the Darlington to Tebay and Penrith lines for many years. 1948 saw the coming of the new LMS-designed 2-6-0s and the beginning of the end of these veterans. Nos 65094 and 65090 (the leading engine fitted with wire and hook for use when banking) stand at Penrith.
Photo: P. B. Whitehouse.

Above: Midhurst, Sussex, 6 March 1948. A train arriving from Petersfield with ex-LBSC D3M class 0-4-4T No 2384 in Southern livery.
Photo: P. M. Alexander.

Below: Swindon-built 0-6-0PT No 7431 with a mixed train on the Bala to Blaenau Festiniog branch near Festiniog on 20 September 1948.
Photo: C. F. H. Oldham.

Above: Ex-A1X class 0-6-0T No 2659 on a Havant to Hayling Island train on 26 June 1948 near Langstone. The loco ex-LBSC No 59, later 659, *Cheam,* built at Brighton in 1875.
Photo: P. M. Alexander.

Below: Guildford 22 October 1948. Class L11 4-4-0 No 438 (Ex-LSWR No 438) on the 12.47pm Reading to Guildford. The number is still on the buffer beam and the word "Southern" on the tender.
Photo: P. M. Alexander.

Above: Ex-LBSC Class K 2-6-0 No 2346 in Southern livery at Guildford on 14 May 1948.
Photo: P. M. Alexander.

Below: Tunbridge Wells West on 28 October 1948. Class E 4-4-0 No 1159 (Ex-SECR No 159) is arriving on a train from Brighton.
Photo: P. M. Alexander.

Upper left: Shalford, 7 May 1948. SECR Class B1
4-4-0 No 1455 on a Redhill to Reading train.
Photo: P. M. Alexander.

Above: Class C2X 0-6-0 No 32547 (Ex-LBSCR
No 547) on a Tunbridge Wells West to Brighton
train via Eridge, near Groombridge Kent on 24
August 1948.
Photo: P. M. Alexander.

Lower left: Ex-SECR F1 class 4-4-0 No 1105
leaving with the 1.15 pm train from Shalford to
Reading on 9 September 1948.
Photo: P. M. Alexander.

Above: Southern N15X 4-6-0 No 32327 *Trevithick* (in the malachite green livery of the SR) with the 12.54 pm Waterloo to Basingstoke passing Byfleet on 24 August 1948.
Photo: P. M. Alexander.

Below: Ex Southern 'King Arthur' class 4-6-0 No 452 *Sir Meliagrance* with the GWR stock of a Portsmouth to Cardiff train near Fareham on 23 October 1948.
Photo: P. M. Alexander.

Upper right: Southern Railway 'Lord Nelson' class 4-6-0 *Howard of Effingham* with the prefix S in front of her number 854 heads the 11.30 am Waterloo to Bournemouth express near Woking on 7 August 1948.
Photo: P. M. Alexander.

Lower right: Southern H15 class 4-6-0 with a down Exeter express near Rockbeare between Honiton and Exeter on 26 June 1948.
Photo: C. F. H. Oldham.

Above: Inverness shed, May 1948. One HR 'Clan' class No 54767 *Clan Mackinnon* was still shedded here at that time.
Photo: P. B. Whitehouse.

Below: Class I3 4-4-2T No 2085 (ex-LBSCR No 85) in Southern livery with modified cab to suit the Eastern section loading gauge entering Brighton station on 19 August 1948.
Photo: P. M. Alexander.

Above: E5X class 0-6-2T No 32576 (ex-LBSCR No 576) in full BR livery at Brighton station on the same date.
Photo: P. M. Alexander.

Below: Ex-GWR 0-6-2T No 394 (Ex-Taff Vale Railway) on a Barry to Cardiff (Riverside) train passing Cardiff General Station on 9 October 1948.
Photo: P. M. Alexander.

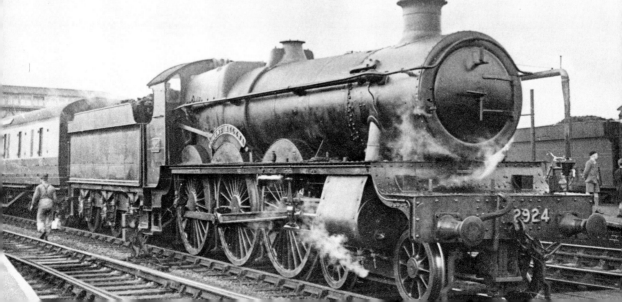

Top left: Ex-GWR 41XX class 2-6-2T No 4119 piloting 38XX 2-8-0 No 3847 on an up goods through the Severn Tunnel on 9 October 1948. Photo: P. M. Alexander.

Above: 'Bulldog' class No 3364 *Frank Bibby* from Westbury stands in Old Oak Common shed in December 1948. Photo: P. M. Alexander.

Bottom left: GWR 'Saint' class 4-6-0 No 2924 *Saint Helena* hooking off a Shrewsbury train at Hereford station on 6 November 1948. The locomotive carries the larger 4000gallon tender and aiong with its coaches it is in full GWR livery. Photo: P. M. Alexander.

Churchdown, Worcestershire, 4 September 1948. GWR 'Star' class 4-6-0 No 4025 (originally *King Charles* and subsequently renamed *Italian Monarch*) on a Birmingham to South Wales express via Gloucester. The locomotive is still in GWR livery, albeit filthy.
Photo: P. M. Alexander.

Bristol: St Philip's Marsh shed, 10 October 1948. GWR 'Saint' class 4-6-0 No 2981 *Ivanhoe* still in her old livery.
Photo: P. M. Alexander.

One of the then few remaining GWR 'Aberdare' class of double-framed 2-6-0s, No 2667, on a South Wales to Birmingham freight (via Gloucester) near Churchdown, Worcestershire on 4 September 1948.
Photo: P. M. Alexander.

Above: GWR No 4017 *Knight of Liege* recently ex-works at Bath station on 14 August 1948.
Photo: P. M. Alexander.

Overleaf: "The Hungry Lion". Proposed British Railways crest for tenders and locos as applied to Western Region "King" class No 6009 *King Charles II* experimentally painted blue, lined in cream red and grey.
Photo: P. C. Short.